NECESSITIES FOR A GOOD RISOTTO: rice

dry wine

cheese

tasty stock in a sturdy pot

a wooden spoon

NECESSITIES FOR A GOOD RISOTTO: rice

butter

dry wine

cheese

tasty stock in a sturdy pot

a wooden spoon

RISOTTO

RISOTTO

A Taste of Milan

Constance Arkin Del Nero
and Rosario Del Nero

ILLUSTRATIONS BY CONSTANCE ARKIN DEL NERO

HARPER & ROW, PUBLISHERS, New York

CAMBRIDGE, PHILADELPHIA, SAN FRANCISCO, LONDON
MEXICO CITY, SÃO PAULO, SINGAPORE, SYDNEY

Designed by Barbara DuPree Knowles

Library of Congress Cataloging-in-Publication Data

Del Nero, Constance.
  Risotto: a taste of Milan.

  Includes index.
  1. Cookery (Rice) 2. Cookery, Italian—Northern style. I. Del Nero, Rosario. II. Title.
TX809.R5D45 1988   641.6′318   88-45112
ISBN 0-06-015913-8

---

88 89 90 91 92 MPC 10 9 8 7 6 5 4 3 2 1

To my father, Arthur Arkin,
who loved to eat

Contents

Fairy Tale Risotti

New Fancies and Old Favorites

Introduction

had just arrived home from work early one Saturday afternoon and was thinking of Rosario and hoping he would call me. (I've just spiraled back in time five years, to gray and steamy Milan, when my husband was an acquaintance whom I dreamed of making my boyfriend, and I was a starry-eyed twenty-three-year-old with a crush as big as any fourteen-year-old's.)

I put water on to boil, inasmuch as I had started to make a simple lunch of *pasta in bianco* (pasta with butter and cheese), when, just as in a second-rate novel, the phone rang. Only this was reality, the caller was Rosario, and I was ecstatic. The reason for the call: an invitation to lunch. The substance of the lunch: risotto. More specifically: *risotto ai carciofi* (risotto with artichokes).

Rosario explained that he couldn't come to pick me up because he had already started the risotto, and as everyone knows, risotto in progress can't be left. No matter, I said; give me directions to come by *metropolitana*—I'm leaving right now. This, of course, was a lie. First I had to change my clothes. Then I had to put on some makeup. Decide whether to wear a belt. Change my clothes again. And then, accompanied by all the usual fears of "I don't look good enough—will he really like me?" mixed with supreme anticipation of the two little kisses on either cheek which Italians always give and which I knew Rosario would give me (and anticipation of the risotto, but let's face it: it did take a back seat in this particular instance), I started toward the *metropolitana*.

I was late, of course. As I hastened down the tree-lined Via Correggio, I could see Rosario leaning on his balcony railing, looking for me. He wasn't being stood up, was he? Not on your life, though I did almost ruin the risotto, which was getting a bit mushy as a result of overcooking—surely ample reason to drop me and look elsewhere for a more respectful girl!

Needless to say, I got my two little kisses and a still-wonderful risotto, which Rosario served with some good Frisun wine from Valtellina.

I'd like to say that I decided to marry Rosario right then and there, but that wouldn't be the truth: I'd decided to marry Rosario the first time I saw him, so there goes that little part of my risotto fairy tale, but no matter. . . . Rosario has since introduced me to many variations on the risotto theme, and between taste-laden mouthfuls, I've often thought they might make a nice subject for a little book. And though it may be a much overused introduction, I know of no better than *buon appetito!*

Why Risotto

Rice, like pasta, is a vehicle—a marvelous, versatile carrier of other flavors, textures, and tastes. And risotto is the king of rice dishes. Perhaps it may best be defined as a Northern Italian specialty that involves cooking rice by the absorption method. In Italy, risotto is a *primo piatto*—a prelude to a meal—but accompanied by a salad and a glass of wine (or two), a generous portion can be a lovely one-dish meal, which is relatively low in cost and certainly nutritious.

When I showed Rosario the first draft of this beginning, he wrinkled up his nose and said, *"Questo non va bene*—this will never do! Nobody is going to want to try a rice dish that takes a good half hour to prepare, and with constant supervision, no less, unless they know what's so special about it. You have to tell people "why risotto," explaining how, in the initial cooking stages, hot butter opens the pores of the rice so that all kinds of good flavors can seep in." Rosario moves his hands over an imaginary pot like a genie, and I truly believe he can smell the fragrance of melting butter. "You have to mention that when you add the wine"—here Rosario makes a liberal wine-adding gesture—"and it hits the pot, it causes vapor, steaming the rice slightly. And you have to tell about the stock: how you add it just a little at a time, so the rice absorbs it slowly. . . ."

By now Rosario is really animated, and I've conjured up a picture of a thousand little grains of rice—all tender, susceptible morsels, ready to absorb a myriad of tastes, each grain a treasure united by a creamy whole. No other way of cooking rice gets similar results.

I hope your nostrils are starting to dilate. And lest you think we speak only about ourselves, let me hasten on to . . .

A Minihistory of Rice,
Followed by the Birth of Risotto

Rice, or "swamp treasure," as it has been called, has a long and, surprisingly, easily traceable history. Consider the word *arisi*, from an Indian language of five thousand years ago. Or *vhrihi* in Sanskrit . . . *brizi* in Persian . . . *rizi* in Greek . . . *oryza* in Latin . . . *riso* in Italian . . . *ris* in Milanese dialect . . . *risotto* in culinary heaven!

Historians estimate that the cultivation of rice began in India in 3000 B.C. and soon spread to China and Africa. In 2800 B.C., a Chinese emperor designed a ceremony to be used during the planting of rice, the principal nutrient of his people. Alexander the Great brought rice to the valleys of the Indus and the Euphrates in the fourth century B.C.

Rice may be an inexpensive staple today, but in Roman times it was a luxury so prohibitively expensive that it wasn't used for food. It was valued for medicinal and cosmetic purposes. Indeed, young slaves with perfect teeth would chew up grains of rice until they were reduced to mush. This paste was then passed on to their mistresses, who valued it as a superlative face mask! Rice continued to be an expensive commodity in the West throughout the Middle Ages. In 1336, the court of Milan fixed its price at twelve crowns per pound—four crowns more per pound than honey—a veritable fortune.

The history of rice in Western cooking began in the seventh century A.D., when the Saracens invaded Spain. The Spanish immediately used it in cooking, and the Aragons brought the tradition of its cultivation with them to Naples in 1442. From there it is easy to follow rice on its trip north to its niche in Lombard cuisine. In fact, by 1465 it was already grown profusely around Milan. In 1475, Galeazzo Sforza gave over one and a half tons of seeds to the duke of Ferrara, in an act of generosity that was followed by reconsideration in the form of a law making it criminal to export rice from the duchy. This law obviously did not instill much fear in the people; soon rice paddies abounded all over the north.

The exact link between the growing of rice and the birth of risotto is a bit fuzzy. The first cookbooks since ancient times, written between 1200 and 1300, were tied to the field of medicine and were written by well-educated men. It would never have crossed anyone's mind then to sing the praises of a culinary delight such as risotto and give directions for recreating it to others. The first signed cookbook of Renaissance times came out in 1475, shortly after the invention of movable type. Its author was Bartholomeo Sacchi, the Lombardy-born librarian of the Vatican. His works were translated into French under the reign of Francis I, whose burning desire it was to get hold of recipes for Italian delicacies. (No wonder he was one of the few to get along with Catherine de' Medici when she came to marry his son in 1533, accompanied by her best Florentine cooks!)

All this still doesn't touch on when and where the first risotto was made; it only lets us know that Renaissance culture was buzzing with interest in the craft of cooking, along with the nobler arts. It seems only logical that the beginning of mass cultivation of rice around Milan, and the new interest in cooking,

gave birth to risotto sometime in the late fifteenth century. For the past two centuries, risotto and risotto-like recipes have abounded.

Choosing a Rice for Risotto

Two things make risotto special. One is good ingredients and the other is proper cooking procedure. Gentle, slow cooking is an important element in the philosophy of risotto, and therefore it is important to use a rice that will stand up to the cooking process and not fall apart or become mushy. A proper risotto should be *all'onda* (literally, wavelike), which is to say that each grain should be slightly al dente but the grains should be held together by a smooth, creamy whole.

The kinds of rice known as *superfini* in Italian, characterized by their big, round grains, are excellent to this end. During cooking, they release surface starch, which envelops the grains and gives the dish its characteristic luscious consistency. A poll of Milanese restaurants that specialize in traditional cooking shows a clear preference for three different types: Two, Arborio and Carnaroli, are *superfini*, but the other, Maratelli, belongs to the *semifini* group, which means that its grains are smaller, though still round and bulging.

Many brands of Italian rice are readily available here in Italian markets and specialty stores, so finding it shouldn't pose a problem. However, if you're far from such places, using Uncle Ben's is acceptable. Because it is parboiled (a special treatment that strengthens the grain as well as locking in natural nutrients), it doesn't break down too much in cooking, which is good. Rosario once fooled a noted food critic into thinking Uncle Ben's was Arborio, which just goes to prove our second point, which is that good cooking is as important as good ingredients. Feel free to experiment with different types of rice.

Necessary Things

◆ THE POT. This, Rosario claims, is what was responsible for his having fooled the aforementioned food critic. "You can have magic rice," he says, "but if you don't have a good pot, you can forget about getting a satisfactory risotto out of the deal." A good risotto pot should be heavy and, if possible, have a copper bottom. The pot should also possess a firm handle that you can hold with one hand while you mix the risotto with the other.

◆ A WOODEN SPOON. A metal spoon will damage both your pot and the tender grains of rice.

◆ BUTTER. Yes. Use the unsalted kind. Don't use margarine or oil.

◆ RICE. (See "Choosing a Rice for Risotto," page 21.)

◆ DRY WINE. (See individual recipes for suggestions.)

◆ STOCK. (See "On Stock," page 26.)

◆ CHEESE. (See "On Cheese," page 23.)

On Cheese

Meet the *grana* family of cheese, sold commercially under the names Parmigiano-Reggiano, Grana Padano, and Grana Lodigiano. *Grana* is so prevalent in Milanese cooking that when one says the word for "cheese" in Milan, one means *grana,* and *grana* it is that takes what might otherwise be an ordinary rice dish and whisks it off to culinary heaven. This wonderful cheese is at least ten centuries old; special references have been made to it since the fifteenth century. In 1567, Ludovico Guicciardini said in his description of commerce in the Netherlands: "From Milan and its province come gold and silver threads, silk cloths of many colors including gold and scarlet, different kinds of rice, armor and haberdashery and also a particular cheese called Parmesan, of great value." Well, two ingredients of risotto had a pretty high standing there.

The various types of *grana* are all made in the same way and take their family name from their grainy texture and their tendency to crumble into minute pieces when grated. In fact, when you chew a little chunk of *grana,* it seems as if there is a grain of sand here and there. Different pastures, and the consequently different cows' milk, are the chief factors for the differences between one type of *grana* and another.

The English word "Parmesan," which would refer to the first of these cheeses, is often used generically when *grana* is meant, but Parmesan is a kind of *grana* and not vice versa. Any kind of *grana* bought by the wedge and grated at the moment you need it is fine for risotto, but stay away from the brightly colored cans and packets of grated cheese found on supermarket shelves. There's a world of difference between them and the real thing. It's a pity they are allowed to share the same name here; in Italy, Parmigiano is a jealously protected designation.

(While I'm telling you to stay away from things, let me also warn you off Romano when thinking risotto. Romano is a grating cheese as well, but it is made at least partially from sheep's milk and has a sharp taste, which would overpower the other ingredients in risotto.)

Grana is made from partially skimmed cow's milk. The milk is treated by an acid fermentation process and then cooked for about half an hour, until the curd separates. The curd then goes into large round forms, where it is dried, drained, pressed, colored, washed, brushed, scraped, and rubbed with oil. Then it's up to time to do its work. Of course, the precious cheeses are kept under constant surveillance, and any problems that arise are promptly taken care of.

Properly cared for, *grana* may keep for up to twenty years, and—like many good wines—it gets better and better.

During the first year of aging, the semifat, firm-fleshed cheese is stored in a damp, cool place. Afterward, it must be sealed from the air with a special coating and placed in a warmer, more humid aging chamber. After two years, the cheese is called *vecchio*, or old; after three years, *stravecchio*, or very old. And after four years, it is known as *stravecchione*—extra old.

A good grating *grana* should be at least two years old, and its surface should be pocked with minute pinpoint holes. Store your *grana* in a brown paper bag with a slightly moistened all-cotton towel around it.

Random Cheese Notes

I know you're groaning about the high cost of real Parmesan cheese, so try to use every little scrap. Scrape the crust well with a knife. Save the hard cleaned crusts to throw into the risotto pot toward the end of the cooking—a common usage in Italy. Rosario and his brother and sisters always hoped it would turn up on their plates.

Grana not branded Parmigiano-Reggiano costs less.

When you use older *grana*, use less: it's stronger.

One of the peculiarities of *grana*: You don't cut a wedge out, as you would with other cheeses; instead you insert a knife and flake off pieces. Special *grana* knives exist for those who wish to "flake" authentically.

In the most elegant restaurants of Milan and vicinity, risotto is served tableside from a hollowed-out half-wheel of *grana*. This exceptional serving "bowl" can be stored in the freezer—it's sure to make an impression at a party; it even makes a one-dish party seem luxurious.

Parmalat, the big Italian dairy, now sells wedges of

Parmesan in convenient Cryovac packages. Distribution is widespread.

On Stock

Risotto is a simple dish, with relatively few ingredients. Consequently, each element gets its share of the limelight and sparkles individually on your palate. The stock you use is important; as the rice swells, it absorbs the stock's flavor. Whenever possible, you should make your own stock. Nothing beats homemade.

Having a supply of homemade stock on hand makes good sense. You can use it not only in risotto but in soups, sauces, and all kinds of wonderful dishes. And best of all, stock is really no trouble to make. You don't have to plan or shop for it. Just save all scraps and bones from chicken, beef, veal, and fish, as well as the shells from shellfish, and store them in separate plastic containers in your freezer. Almost nothing is too lowly for the stock pot—even vegetable parings can go in. Once you have filled one of the containers, you're ready to make stock.

Place the contents of the container in a tall, narrow pot. Cover with cold water and place over a low flame. Allow the stock to simmer for three to four hours. Then strain it, cool slightly, and refrigerate it, covered, until the fat congeals.

If you want to store the stock for future use, simply remove and discard the layer of fat and pour the stock into a plastic container for freezing. Be sure to leave room for expansion. Also, it's wise to label and date the container. Frozen stock will stay good for several months. If you have limited room in your freezer, you may want to reduce the stock to a glaze, for easier storage: After you have removed the fat, simmer the stock until you have reduced it to a concentrated semiliquid. When you use it, just reconstitute with water.

If you plan to use the stock within the next few days, simply leave the layer of fat undisturbed and the stock will keep nicely in the fridge. Should you remove the fat layer, or should it become broken, bring the stock to a boil, let it simmer for at least ten minutes, cool, and return to the refrigerator.

If the stock is cloudy and you wish to clarify it, follow these easy steps: Cover the bottom of a pot with clean celery leaves. Add one beaten egg per quart of stock. Then pour in the cold stock. Bring it slowly to a boil and wait for the egg to rise to the top. There is no need to stir unless the egg starts to stick to the bottom of the pot. When the egg has risen, filter the stock, through cheesecloth, into another pot.

You don't have to have stock on hand if you plan your second course with the risotto in mind. The preparation involved in making simple yet tasty dishes such as vitello tonnato, bollito misto, or poached salmon leaves you a flavored water that is already halfway to being homemade stock. Use it for making risotto.

Even so, the day will come when you will need to make stock from scratch, and you don't have anything put away in your containers. You can use the following guidelines in that case.

◆ FOR CHICKEN STOCK. Place approximately three pounds of chicken bones—with or without meat—and any scraps you may have, in a high, narrow pot. Use wings, legs, backs, or entire carcasses. Organs—omit livers—are good too. Add two carrots, two stalks of celery, and one ripe tomato, cut in half. Make an "onion apple" by taking a large onion, a bay leaf, and a clove, and attaching the bay leaf to the onion, using the clove as a nail. Once the stock is ready, this handy seasoning unit is easy to remove without having to hunt for little pieces in the pot. Cover all ingredients with approximately six quarts of cold water and bring to a boil. Then turn the heat down to a simmer and cook covered for about four hours.

You may want to add ½ cup white wine, a couple of cloves of garlic, and/or a few whole peppercorns. You can round out the flavor by adding some vegetarian broth or a vegetarian bouillon cube. Let the stock cool and strain through cheesecloth. Then follow storage directions or, if you intend to use it the same day, lift off and discard the layer of fat.

◆ FOR BEEF STOCK. Use 1½ pounds beef bones and 1½ pounds meat. Muscular cuts, such as leg, neck, or back meat, release the most flavor. Add a couple of ripe tomatoes, cut in half, as well as two carrots, two stalks of celery, and an "onion apple" (see directions under chicken stock, above). Add about six quarts cold water and bring to a boil. Turn the heat down so the stock simmers, and cook covered for about four hours. Remove bones and strain the stock through cheesecloth.

◆ FOR VEAL STOCK. Ask your butcher for three pounds of veal leg and shank bones with meat attached, cut into three- to four-inch pieces. Place them in the soup pot, together with a stalk of celery, a carrot, and an "onion apple" (see directions under chicken stock, above). Add ½ cup white wine and six quarts cold water. Heat to a boil and then reduce to a simmer. Cook covered for four hours before removing bones and straining.

A note on veal stock: This is called for in a very delicate risotto, where a stronger stock might overpower some of the subtler flavors.

◆ FOR FISH STOCK. Place about four pounds fish bones and trimmings (include heads and tails—your fish merchant can give you these) in a soup pot. Add two quarts cold water, one cup white wine, two cloves garlic, a tomato cut in half, and an "onion apple" (see directions under chicken stock, on the facing page).

Mix in a handful of fresh parsley and four sprigs of fresh thyme (you can substitute ½ teaspoon dried thyme leaves). If you have shrimp shells or lobster bodies, by all means add them to the pot. Any water that you've used for steaming clams or mussels is also a welcome addition. Bring your pot of goodies to a boil, give it a stir, and then lower the heat to a simmer.

Cook covered for about a half hour, mixing occasionally. Remove bones and all solids with a slotted spoon, then strain, cook, and refrigerate covered in an airtight container. Freeze the fish stock if you don't plan to use it within two days.

> 4 *tablespoons (½ stick) butter*
> 2 *cloves garlic, cut in half*
> 1 *tablespoon chopped parsley*
> 4 *medium zucchini, cut in wedges*
> 6–8 *mushrooms, cut in thick slices*
> 1 *large white unpeeled onion, cut in half*
> 2 *bay leaves*
> 2 *cloves*
> 5–6 *unpared carrots, scrubbed and cut in half*
> 1 *medium bunch celery, separated into stalks*
> 2 *large plum tomatoes, cut in half*
> *Pinch sea salt (omit if you use salted butter)*

Melt the butter in a soup pot over medium heat. Add the garlic, parsley, zucchini, and mushrooms, and sauté gently, without letting the ingredients brown. Grill or broil the onion halves until they start to burn on the edges; attach a bay leaf to each half, using the cloves as nails. Put the onion, carrots, celery, and tomatoes into the stock pot, cover with 5–6 quarts cold water, add the sea salt, and bring to a boil. Reduce the heat so the stock simmers and cook covered for two hours. Strain the stock through cheesecloth and use or store.

How to Eat Risotto

If making risotto is a science, eating it is too. Risotto should always be nice and hot. Italians take care that it remains the right temperature while they eat by serving it in wide bowls. They place a mound of risotto in the middle and gently spread the rice out toward the edges with their forks. Then they eat a ring around their risotto, after which they spread more rice out from the mound toward the edges of the bowl. This procedure is repeated until all the risotto is gone. The rice in the center mound stays nice and hot because of its thickness, and the rice on the thinner edges cools off just enough not to burn your mouth.

The real old Milanese believe that risotto should be eaten with a spoon. If you opt for a particularly soupy risotto (but be careful—the grains themselves should always be a bit al dente), you may want to use a spoon too.

About the Recipes

The fifteen risotti in this book are presented under three headings. Family Risotti traditionally find their place on the Del Nero table at different times of the year. Fairy Tale Risotti are preceded by historical lore. And New Fancies and Old Favorites are just that: some classics, some experiments—in short, too good to leave out.

Special notes on the ingredients, as well as wine suggestions and descriptions, follow each recipe.

Each recipe will serve up four healthy platefuls or six appetizers.

Family
Risotti

RISOTTO AI CARCIOFI

Risotto with Artichokes

> *Approximately 6–8 cups chicken stock*
> *4 artichokes*
> *Juice of 1 lemon*
> *8 tablespoons (1 stick) butter*
> *1 medium white onion, cut in small pieces*
> *2 cups raw rice*
> *¾ cup Vernaccia di San Gimignano wine*
> *12 crushed green peppercorns*
> *¾ cup grated Parmesan cheese (grana, see page 23)*

Bring a large pot of chicken stock to a boil on a burner at the back of the stove. Once it starts to bubble, lower the flame to a whisper. Keep the stock nice and hot, but not actively boiling, while making risotto.

Cut off and discard the top third and all spiny leaf tips from each artichoke. Quarter the remaining portions, and carefully remove the entire bristly choke using a sharp knife. Squeeze the juice from the lemon into a small container of water, and drop the artichoke quarters in to keep them from turning brown. Cut each piece into thickish slices (this way they will remain al dente when the risotto is served) and return to the water until ready to use.

Melt six tablespoons (¾ stick) butter in the risotto pot over a low flame. Add the onion and sauté until it loses all its color and becomes limp. Toss in the artichoke slices and give them a chance to bathe in the onion butter. Then add the rice and turn up the flame slightly, to give the rice a toasting. This *tostatura* is one of the keys to a good risotto; it provokes a chemical change in the surface starch and ensures separate grains with a creamy consistency.

Pour in the Vernaccia, stir, and let it steam away. Add a cupful of simmering chicken stock, mix well, and wait for the rice to absorb it while stirring often. Then add a second cupful, stir, and wait for the pot to absorb it too. Repeat this procedure, stirring frequently, until the rice is almost tender but firm to the bite. Then, along with the last cupful of stock, throw in the peppercorns, stir, and taste often to test for doneness. The risotto is done when the rice is just barely tender but still al dente. This should take 20–25 minutes. Then turn off the flame, and add the last two tablespoons butter and the grated *grana*. Cover for a minute or two, and serve immediately, with extra cheese available on the table.

The rest of the Vernaccia, nicely chilled, will be most *gradito** with the risotto.

Artichoke Notes

Look for firm, closed artichokes when you go to the market. Avoid those that are opened, are yellowed, or have loose leaves.

You may find it easy to use a kitchen scissors to cut off the pointy tips on the artichoke leaves.

*Pleasing.

A WORD ABOUT *Vernaccia*

Vernaccia is a pale gold wine that has long been made around the tiny hilltop town of San Gimignano in Tuscany. Its clean, flowery taste calls to mind bright Italian sunshine, soft green rolling hills, and the dreamy warmth of Perugino landscapes.

OTHER SUGGESTED WINES: Monte Antico Bianco (Tuscany), Albana di Romagna (Emilia-Romagna), or Chardonnay (Tuscany, Emilia-Romagna, or Friuli).

THE PORCINI GODDESS

Rosario's mother, Rosaria, had fallen down the stairs the day before and badly twisted her ankle. It was all puffed up, with highly colored bruises, and resembled an overripe peach. In short, a nasty business. She had it propped up on the coffee table and was contemplating it.

"*Domani vado a funghi*" (Tomorrow I'm going to pick mushrooms), she said decisively. (*Funghi* simply means mushrooms in Italian, but to someone from Morbegno, in the Valtellina, northern Lombardy, *funghi* means porcini, the only—local—mushrooms worth eating.)

"But how can you?" I asked. "You can hardly walk!"

"Well, I must," she replied. "The moon is right, the humidity is right. There'll be tons of mushrooms out all over the mountains, and just as many people looking for them. I'm going to get up at five."

I didn't hear Rosaria leave, but when I, your typical sleepyhead, got up at nine o'clock and came downstairs, she was already back, examining her find. Two huge baskets heaped high with porcini were on the kitchen table. Some of the mushrooms were as small as your pinkie toe—others were as large as a coffee mug.

She was happy to talk about her early-morning adventure, and I soon felt myself walking with her in a little field. A large number of other early risers were walking about on the flat land. No challenge for her there, so she slipped off into the woods where the ground begins to slope down. At a certain point there is a sharp drop, and this is where Rosaria decided there must be *funghi*. She held on to a tree and let herself slide a bit, reaching the ledge three feet down. After she steadied herself and rearranged her hold, she looked around carefully. Two *funghi* off to the right. One down on the left. Then she probed the area directly under the miniledge. Sure enough! A whole family of porcini!

"They like to grow in out-of-the-way places," she explained.

And then she winced a bit. Just a bit, because Rosaria is the kind of dynamic person who will defeat pain.

"Your ankle!" I remembered. "What about your ankle?"

"Oh, it's okay," she answered.

I must not have looked convinced, because she then added, "Look—when it's time to go for *funghi*, it's time to go for *funghi*. No sense letting everybody else snap them up."

Rosaria's ankle swelled purple over the white fur-lined slipper she reposed it in. She slid me a slice of just cleaned porcino, and as I slowly nibbled it I began to see her point.

I told Rosaria that I'd like to accompany her on her next porcini mission. Accordingly, a sissy jaunt was organized. We left at noon and walked through tame-looking meadows. No treacherous cliffs for me. Rosaria explained that there was no sense at all in taking an amateur on a serious hunt. All the same, we found a few porcini scattered round. A middle-aged gentleman who seemed to be about the same business eyed a porcini threesome nestled together at exactly the same time as Rosaria. "Ah, signora . . ." he said, with a note of renunciation in his voice, and let her take them. "Not much at this hour." "No, no," she exclaimed. "It's much too late."

Even so, every few minutes she would launch a cry of *"Un fungo! Un fungo!"* and little by little her basket filled up, though it was substantially smaller than the basket she carried when she meant serious business.

My porcini lesson did not stop with the field trip, however. When we got home, Rosaria showed me how to inspect the mushrooms. The perfect ones, which show no sign of having been eaten by worms or snails, get marinated and stored *sott'olio* (in olive oil) in mason jars. Properly done, they will keep indefinitely, and in fact they can be found on Rosaria's table on a special occasion at any time of year.

At least 80 percent of a day's crop are filled with myriad pin-sized holes. Food for the discriminating insect! These porcini get sliced and set out on the terrace, to begin the process of sun and air drying. After a month or so, they are put away in plastic bags for storage, and anytime the kids want an extra-special risotto, the porcini get taken out and revived in water.

A recipe using dried porcini appears on page 48.

The following recipe is for risotto with fresh mushrooms. I have a couple of friends who have found porcini growing in Massachusetts, but unless you know your mushrooms, I would suggest you settle for *Agaricus bisporus*, known in Italian supermarkets as champignons and in American ones (for lack of cultivated competition) as mushrooms. ◆◆

RISOTTO AI FUNGHI FRESCHI

Risotto with Fresh Mushrooms

> 12 *medium-sized mushrooms*
> *Approximately 6–8 cups beef stock or*
>   *mixed meat stock*
> 8 *tablespoons (1 stick) butter*
> 1 *medium white onion, cut in half-inch squares*
> 2 *cups raw rice*
> ¾ *cup Pinot Grigio wine*
> ¾ *cup grated Parmesan cheese* (grana)
> 2 *tablespoons chopped fresh parsley*

Clean the mushrooms. Separate the stems from the caps and add to the stock. Bring the stock to a boil and let simmer for a good thirty minutes before starting to make risotto. (If you're making stock from scratch, add the stems along with the other vegetables.) Keep the stock on very low heat throughout the risotto procedure.

Cut the caps into thin, even slices. Set aside.

Place six tablespoons (¾ stick) butter in the risotto pot and warm over a low flame until melted. Add the chopped onion and stir well until transparent. Next, add the rice, increase the heat slightly, and stir well to coat with the hot butter. When the rice shines like sparkling jewels, pour the Pinot Grigio over it, mix, and let it sizzle until the alcohol evaporates. Ladle a cupful of hot stock over the rice, and wait for the rice to absorb it while stirring often. Then ladle over another cupful of stock, mix, and wait until the rice

absorbs it, stirring frequently. Continue the procedure until the rice is midway to doneness (10–12 minutes).

Spread the sliced mushroom caps over the rice and
fold into the risotto. Continue ladling over the stock,
mixing thoroughly, and waiting for the rice to absorb
it until the risotto is al dente (another 8–10 minutes).
Turn off the flame, mix in the grated cheese, parsley,
and remaining two tablespoons butter. Cover for a
minute or two, and serve.

As always, have extra cheese available on the table
for the *golosi*.* The rest of the Pinot Grigio, cool and
crisp, is the perfect complement.

Fresh Mushroom Notes

Many mushrooms are sprayed with an antioxidant to
keep them from turning brown as they age. Look for
mushrooms that have dirt clinging to their stems:
They usually haven't been tampered with and are
worth the extra trouble it takes to clean them.

You can slice mushroom caps quickly and uniformly
using an egg slicer.

To clean mushrooms, wash them lightly and swiftly
with a soft brush under running water, then shake
well if using immediately or pat dry with a dish towel
for later use.

*Gourmands.

A WORD ABOUT *Pinot Grigio*

Pinot Grigio comes from the northeastern region of Friuli, which borders on Austria and Yugoslavia. Alpine and Adriatic intermingle to produce a hospitable wine-growing climate. *Colli orientali* (the easternmost hills) have the most favorable conditions. Styles of Pinot Grigio range from a light yellow wine with a cool grayish tinge and crisp fruit, to a smoky, coppery one with richer body and aroma. The unusual attractive color of this last style predisposes one in its favor before one even raises the glass!

OTHER SUGGESTED WINES: Tocai, Pinot Bianco, Chardonnay (all Friuli).

THE TREASURE AT THE TOP OF
THE WORLD TRADE CENTER

osaria flew into Boston, and her first contact with the United States was flashy Route 1, with its gargantuan restaurants in the strangest of shapes —a red ship, the Leaning Tower of Pisa, a carousel— and an unlikely string of motels. A half hour's drive brought us to Essex, a town of 2,000, where my mother lives, the ideal place to recover from jet lag and find one's bearings. Snow fell daily and isolated us from reality.

A week slipped by, and Rosario and I took his mother to see Gloucester harbor and slumbering Rockport, with only a fraction of its gift shops open, its waterfront restaurants with their generous windows affording views of ice chunks, brave ducks, and a rare seal. At night we lit a fire, tried to play Scrabble in Italian but realized the letter distribution was all wrong, and generally went to bed early. One evening caught Rosaria wondering out loud where the America that she knew was. To many a foreigner's vision, America means huge skyscrapers vying with each other to scratch higher up into the sky: wall-to-wall buildings, gray and glass, stretching as far as the eye can see.

Rosario consulted with me, and we planned a surprise trip to New York. I called my brother, who still has our family apartment there, one of those eight-room rent-controlled Upper West Side rarities. Two days later, we drove into Rosaria's America.

Our first morning dawned cold, but time was at

a premium, so we bundled up and announced a tour of Midtown. We spent a lot of time on Fifth Avenue, people-watching and shop-browsing. Into Rizzoli's for an Italian newspaper, and then on down to Rockefeller Center. The novelty of New York outweighed the biting cold, but before we'd gone another ten blocks, Rosaria let it be known in short, steamy breaths that she'd love a cup of hot coffee. We found a Greek deli and talked over what to do next. Down and over to Macy's? Up and over to Bloomingdale's? No, Rosaria wasn't interested in stores. She wanted panorama.

The World Trade Center was in order then, and I directed us toward the IRT, while telling Rosaria much of what she could expect to see.

Half an hour later, we were gathered in front of the big elevator. On the ride up, our ears popped faster than champagne corks on New Year's Eve. Our stomachs suddenly landed in our throats, signaling we were *there.*

Rosaria walked from window to window and took in the view. The steely blue and gray of streets and buildings spread uptown, punctuated by yellow dots: taxicabs. We noticed a few planes below us. "It's beautiful," Rosaria breathed, as she stood mesmerized by the changing pattern of traffic on the backdrop of Manhattan. She was taking in New York, and it was a heady experience.

She finally tore herself away, and we went over to look at the exhibit on the inside walls. Here, in A–Z fashion, was arranged a sort of minihistory of the world. Each letter stood for some aspect of humanity, culture, or history. Rosaria, her head buzzing with the new sights, sounds, and experiences of the past few days, went over to look at the first panel. "A" is for "Antipasto," it began, and Rosaria burst out laughing.

Here, at the top of one of the highest buildings in the world in one of the biggest cities in the world, at the beginning of a concise summary of world achievements, was a huge jar of *funghi* from Morbegno! Perfect little porcini sandwiched closely with artichoke hearts and packaged by one of the foremost families of Morbegno . . .

It was too perfect an ending to our World Trade Center visit; we passed up the opportunity to finish the alphabetical history, and headed over to the elevator. *"Volete?"* asked Rosario, taking some chewing gum out of his pocket. "For the trip down."

We all chewed furiously in the elevator and, not surprisingly, thought more or less simultaneously of dinner. "Why don't I make some risotto for your brother to try tonight?" asked Rosaria.

As soon as we were home, she busied herself in the kitchen. I was busy chopping an onion when she excused herself for a moment. "I need something from my suitcase."

She reappeared in a short time with a cellophane packet tied up with a pretty ribbon. Most people bring gold, leather, liquor, or perfume from abroad. Rosaria had brought porcini! I should have known that she would wait for the right moment to produce her treasure. Just as I should have known that when Rosaria says "risotto," the words "with porcini" are understood. ◆◆

RISOTTO AI FUNGHI SECCHI

Risotto with Dried Mushrooms

> 2 ounces (60 grams) dried porcini mushrooms
>   (about 1 cup)
> About 6 cups beef stock
> 8 tablespoons (1 stick) butter
> 1 medium white onion, cut in ½-inch squares
> 4 leaves fresh sage
> 2 cups raw rice
> ¾ cup Valtellina Rosso wine
> 3 tablespoons chopped fresh parsley
> ¾ cup grated Parmesan cheese (grana)

Place the porcini in two cups lukewarm water and soak for half an hour. Then gently lift them out of the water, but do not disturb any of the settlement at the bottom. Some little stones and sand—mushroom habitat, in short—will have collected there. Don't throw out this water! It is precious liquid. Strain it carefully through cheesecloth, and set aside for later addition to the pot.

Set the beef stock on a secondary burner to boil. Once it has started to bubble, lower the heat considerably, but keep it hot for the rest of the procedure.

Melt six tablespoons (¾ stick) butter in the risotto pot over a gentle flame. Add the onion squares and sage leaves; stir. When the onion is soft and just starting to brown, add the rice and raise the heat a grade. Toss the grains to coat well with the sage butter.

Pour in the wine; let it tinge the rice and steam away.

Stir to make sure the rice doesn't stick. Then add the mushrooms and, almost immediately afterward, the strained mushroom water. Blend everything together, using the wooden spoon. Once the mushroom water has been absorbed, add the first cupful of hot beef stock. This, too, should be stirred carefully through the rice and given time to be absorbed. As the stock gets absorbed, add another cupful, never allowing the pot to get too dry. Be sure to stir frequently. Continue to add stock, a cupful at a time, stirring, until the rice is almost tender.

Remove the pot from the flame and swirl in the chopped parsley, grated cheese, and remaining two tablespoons butter. Cover the pot and give it a couple of minutes' rest. Serve it immediately, with extra cheese on the table, *come al solito.**

The rest of the Valtellina Rosso, having had a chance to breathe while the risotto cooked, is a lovely accompaniment. *Che profumo!*+

Dried Mushroom Notes

Imported dried porcini are easily found here in the United States. You may want to try experimenting with other dried wild mushrooms, such as shiitake and chanterelles. Flavor intensifies with drying, so you won't need many to make an exotic "mushroom" statement.

*As usual.

+What a lovely smell!

When you buy dried mushrooms, look for packets containing slices from the cap. Inferior brands tend to use more slices from the stem.

A WORD ABOUT *Valtellina Rosso*

Pretty, mountain-enclosed Valtellina (Lombardy) is the home of ancient vineyards where the Nebbiolo grape thrives, and winemakers make ruby-brick reds with names like Inferno and Paradiso. Along with Sassella, Grumello, and Valgella, these Valtellina Superiore wines contain a minimum 95 percent Nebbiolo grapes. The basic Valtellina Rosso is made throughout the zone with at least 70 percent Nebbiolo. The wines range from slightly tannic to soft and mellow, with woodsy undertones of strawberries and hazelnuts. Terraced mountain plots, which look like cornrows on a green head, receive a coolish sun. Above them, white-capped cousins tell Alpine tales. In the nearby woods, secrets abound.

OTHER SUGGESTED WINES: Any of the Valtellina Superiore wines mentioned above, or Gattinara, Ghemme, Carema (all Piedmont), or other Nebbiolo wines.

BUON ANNO!

The clock is about to strike twelve. Rosario is poised with a bottle of champagne. All Italy pops the cork as the new year begins; toasts and resolutions are forming on the tongue. Pfft! And the cork is snug in Rosario's hand. (It doesn't fly off and hit me in the head the way it did five years ago, before I'd even met Rosario. One of my friends instantly congratulated me: "You'll be married within the year!" "What on earth?" I retorted, rubbing the tender spot on my forehead. "I like living alone. Besides, I don't know anyone I'd spend a weekend with, much less marry!" Wily wisdom in champagne. I won't doubt you anymore!)

"What shall we toast to?" I ask. The answer from Rosario: "Why don't we toast the people who made our book possible?" Another mystery for me. Answer it, champagne. "In 1971, the town of Novara erected a statue to honor all the women who spent their lives bent over, working in the rice paddies. Machinery had only recently replaced them. Once upon a time, the Arborio on your table was the true fruit of their labor. They were little better than slaves. Now they've officially passed into folklore."

Our glasses clink. Starry-eyed, we gaze out our window in a fit of fifties sentimentality. At least we're in sync. Our neighbor's TV is on full blast. She's having a party. The illuminated ball has fallen from its perch in Times Square. People are milling around in scrunched circles; it can't be more fun than a subway car at rush hour. Suddenly, the camera abandons all the revelers, in favor of bells and horn blowers. "Auld Lang Syne" accompanies.

On this border between New Year's Eve and New Year's Day, when we remember the past and dream of the future, Rosario teaches me a new song. One of the many "Rice Paddy Blues" songs, now kept alive in country restaurants that offer weekend entertainment to celebrate risotto: *risotto alla birra* (risotto with beer) . . . *risotto allo champagne* (risotto with champagne) . . .

A way of life has vanished. A nightmare is a memory is a piece of folklore is a party. The songs of the rice paddies are many, these true Italian blues. I've picked just one:

Cara Mamma Vienimi Incontro

O Cara Mamma vienimi incontro
che ho tante cose da raccontar
che nel parlare mi fan tremare
la brutta vita che ho passa'.

La brutta vita che ho passato
La' sul trapianto e nella monda
La mia bella faccia rotonda
Come prima non la vedi piu'.

Alla mattina i moscerini
che mi succhiavano tutto quel sangue
a mezzogiorno quel brutto sole
che mi faceva abbrustolir.

A mezzogiorno fagioli e riso
alla sera riso e fagioli

e quel pane non naturale
che l'appetito ti fa mancar.

Alle nove la ritirata
alle dieci l'ispezione
l'ispezione ma del padrone
tutte in branda a riposar.

Oh, Dear Mamma, Come to Meet Me

Oh, dear Mamma, come to meet me—
I've so many stories to tell;
When I speak I start to shiver,
thinking of the hard life I've led.

What a hard life I've been leading,
a-working and a-weeding,
And my pretty round face
alas is round no more.

There were gnats in the morning,
sucking out our blood,
And the scorching noontime sun
burned and burned and burned.

For lunch we had but beans and rice,
for dinner rice and beans,
served up with some tasteless bread:
True hunger-stopper, that!

At nine o'clock 'twas time for bed
and ten inspection time—
Inspection by the boss man
We're a-dreaming in our cots.

(Translation by Constance Arkin Del Nero) ◆◆

RISOTTINO ALLO CHAMPAGNE

Little Risotto with Champagne

This is a lovely, delicate risotto, which requires light flavors that don't overpower it.

> *Approximately 6–8 cups veal stock*
> *6 tablespoons (¾ stick) butter*
> *½ cup chopped fresh shallots*
> *2 cups raw rice*
> *1¼ cups Italian Prosecco (any brut sparkling wine*
> *   may be used, but don't use anything with even a*
> *   hint of sweetness)*
> *1 tablespoon heavy cream*
> *¾ cup grated Parmesan cheese* (grana)—*preferably*
> *   not too aged*

Bring a potful of stock to boil on a back burner, then turn down the heat to low, and keep at an even simmer throughout the entire risotto procedure.

Place the butter in the risotto pot; melt over a low flame. Add the shallots, stir, and sauté until they are soft to the touch of a wooden spoon. Add the rice, increase the flame, and stir, to coat well with the shallot butter. When the rice looks like shining pearls, pour in one cup of the Prosecco. Let it bubble away; mix carefully. Then ladle over a cupful of stock. Stir while the rice slowly absorbs it, add another ladleful, and stir again, until the stock is absorbed. Continue the add-stir-wait process until the rice is almost done (al dente)—tender to the bite.

Mix in the remaining ¼ cup Prosecco, and swirl it through the risotto. After another minute or so, turn off the flame, add the heavy cream and the grated *grana*, cover, and let sit for a couple of minutes. (You may omit the heavy cream if the risotto is on the soupy side.)

With a last parting mix, it's ready to serve. Have more grated cheese handy, should anyone want it. The remaining Prosecco, served well chilled in flute glasses, is sure to *far scena*.*

A WORD ABOUT *Prosecco*

Prosecco whispers: delicate, dry, light, bubbly, festive, seductive, elegant. It's pale white in color, with the lightest of gold highlights; subtle fruity overtones soften its dryness, the way the tiniest drop of warmth changes an icy white to cream. It has the controlled opulence of Veronese frescoes; and, like the painter, it was born in Veneto.

WINES YOU MAY SUBSTITUTE: Any dry sparkling wine.

*Create an impression.

## AN EPIPHANY

O kay."

"Whoops!"

"No, no . . . wait a minute."

Rosaria and I hoisted the Christmas tree and stead-ied it in a vertical position. We hung a number of ornaments, mostly in friendly silence; Rosaria is not the type to make small talk. Occasionally she stopped to tell me that this ornament was made of dough and came from South America or that that ornament had been in the family for twenty years.

We got to the lights and strung them with care, trying to distribute them evenly, not quite succeed-ing. I told her that in the United States we often strung popcorn and cranberries as a low-cost colorful garland. She liked the idea and said that popcorn reminded her of snowflakes.

After securing a mustard-colored papier-mâché star to the top of the tree, we were ready to devote our attention to the crèche. She had a lovely set of ceramic figurines, and we arranged them around the bottom of the tree, taking care that the scene they composed would be easily seen from any angle. How dearly crafted were the little figurines! What anthro-pomorphizing human had imagined the beatific expressions of the cows and sheep! Gentle smiles il-luminated their beast faces. They were truly aware of a special secret. My favorite of them all was a little donkey, whose legs were crossed oh, so daintily and encircled with delicate wisps of hay. . . .

I shall now be an old-fashioned film director, ripping pages from a calendar and having them fly off into the distance in an unusual rush of wind, as a way of manipulating time, showing its passage.

Christmas, and Rosario's sister Barbara's birthday passes. Her cake, with chocolate curls and a dusting of confectioner's sugar, is completely gone. New Year's Eve, and Rosario's sister Sabrina's wedding anniversary, with its supper of lentils and *zampone* (pork sausage), comes and goes. We get but quick glimpses of the festivities.

Now the pages have stopped disappearing into the upper right of my screen, and we are in a new present. Rosaria is wearing a different dress, but the setting is the same. It's January 6—the day of the Epiphany. This is the last of the great church festivals until Easter; it commemorates the coming of the Magi to Bethlehem. After today, the crèche will be dismantled and put back in its box for another year-long slumber. I secretly wonder if the little animal smiles will disappear, if they will close their adoring eyes.

The tree will be de-decorated and set out in the cold, with an odd strand of tinsel left on here and there to tug at some overly sentimental passerby's heartstrings. Yes, after today a period of hard times, accentuated by long days of gray weather, will set in. The Italians, ever ready with a proverb, say, *"L'Epifania tutte le feste le porta via"* (Epiphany takes all the other holidays with it). On this last night of celebration, there is still an aura of luxury presiding over the table. On this special night, the typical dinner starts with risotto ai fegatini. A last bit of heaven before penance? ◆◆

RISOTTO AI FEGATINI

Risotto with Chicken Livers

> *Approximately 6–8 cups chicken stock*
> *8 tablespoons (1 stick) butter*
> *1 medium white onion, cut in small squares*
> *1 pound chicken livers*
> *2 cups raw rice*
> *½ cup dry Marsala wine*
> *¾ cup grated Parmesan cheese* (grana)
> *2 tablespoons chopped fresh parsley*

Heat the chicken stock to a boil on a back burner, then keep at a simmer on low heat throughout the procedure.

Place six tablespoons (¾ stick) butter in the risotto pot; melt over a lowish flame. Add onion squares and sauté until they become transparent. Stir in the chicken livers and mix till they are almost cooked; remove with a slotted spoon, and set aside.

Raise the flame to medium heat and add the rice. Stir carefully. After a minute of cooking, when the rice is well polished with the butter, add the dry Marsala and stir again. The original Sicilian Marsala is far superior to American imitations, which tend to be too sweet. A number of good brands are easily available and well worth the extra cost.

When the rice has absorbed the Marsala, add a cupful of hot chicken stock and stir often until absorbed. Then mix in a second cupful. Keep your eye on the pot, stirring from time to time, and watching as the rice swells slowly with the stock. When most of the liquid is gone, add another measure of stock and stir often until absorbed. Continue this procedure until the rice is close to done. It should be almost tender but still firm to the bite.

Add the chicken livers once again and give the pot a healthy stir. Remove it from the flame and add the grated *grana*, parsley, and last two tablespoons butter. Swirl through the rice and then cover for a last minute's settling and flavor heightening. Uncover and serve right away. Extra *grana*, anyone?

Eh sì, eh? And *magari** a nice bottle of Merlot too!

A WORD ABOUT *Merlot*

Much good Merlot is produced in Northern Italy, notably in Friuli, Veneto, Trentino, Emilia-Romagna, and Lombardy (Oltrepò Pavese). It is a soft and supple wine, both grapy and herby. Most Merlot is made to be drunk in one to four years, although some vintners prefer to age it, producing a most attractive wine with a pronounced bouquet.

OTHER SUGGESTED WINES: Franciacorta Rosso (Lombardy), Cabernet (Veneto and Friuli), Decugnano dei Barbi Rosso (Umbria), Quarto Vecchio, or Castello di Roncade (both Veneto).

*Perhaps.

Fairy Tale
Risotti

A RENAISSANCE MASTERPIECE

Risotto alla Milanese, *Risott a la Milanesa* to the inhabitants of Milan, celebrates its 414th anniversary this year. A pretty little legend marks its origins. It so happens that in 1572, a Fleming by the name of Valerius van Diependaele, descendant of a family of glaziers from Louvain, arrived in Milan to take up work on the cathedral. His task was to depict the life of Saint Helen in stained glass. At a time when the rest of Italy was caught up in the grand style of the High Renaissance, with its preoccupation with spatial relationships, stained glass had been largely abandoned, as a medium lacking depth. It was only in Milan that the Gothic lived on with any importance, thus making artistic (and indirectly culinary) history.

Valerius had a zealous student with a passion for golden yellow in his work. The young man, to this day anonymous, was nicknamed Zafferano (Saffron) by his contemporaries, because it was with this powder that he imbued his work with its special golden glow. His teacher lovingly admonished him for overusing it, saying, "Methinks, young man, one day you'll forget yourself and mix the stuff in with your food!"

Young Zafferano went about his work, perhaps with a grumble, perhaps not, but the color yellow continued to predominate. Work on the cathedral progressed, and though it's not known exactly how well Valerius and Zafferano got on, it seems that the student and Valerius's daughter soon reached an understanding. They were wed in 1574, amidst much pomp. An elaborate feast was planned, and the other apprentices didn't lose the opportunity to play a happy joke. That day, a certain rice dish had its place on the menu. While the pot was bubbling merrily, one of the young men slipped a bit of saffron in with the other ingredients, and a heavenly dish with a distinctive golden aura was born. Today you can find it in any *trattoria milanese*. ◆◆

RISOTTO ALLA MILANESE

(Risotto with Veal Marrow and Saffron)

> *Approximately 6–8 cups beef or mixed meat stock*
> *6 tablespoons (¾ stick) butter*
> *1 medium white onion, cut in small pieces*
> *1 tablespoon veal marrow*
> *2 cups raw rice*
> *¾ cup Lugana wine*
> *Pinch saffron, or one (¹²⁄₁₀₀ gram) Italian packet*
> *   saffron*
> *¾ cup grated Parmesan cheese* (grana)

Set the stock to heat on a back burner. Keep it hot, but not boiling, throughout the entire procedure.

Melt five tablespoons butter in the risotto pot. Spread the chopped onion over the bottom of the pot and stir gently until it becomes transparent.

Add the veal marrow; mix well.

Add the rice, increase the heat a bit, and stir till all the grains are glossy with the marrow butter. Pour in the Lugana, mix, and let it steam for a few seconds. When the wine is almost gone, add the first cupful of hot stock and mix. Wait for this to be absorbed while stirring often, then add another cupful of hot stock. Continue doling out the stock and stirring, until the rice is ever so slightly chewy.

Dissolve the saffron in ½ cup of stock. Once the rice is almost tender pour the saffron stock over the risotto and give a good stir. (If you add the saffron directly to the pot, the rice will not be homogeneously colored.) The saffron reaches peak flavor in just a couple of minutes, so make sure you don't add it too soon.

Take the pot off the flame, add the remaining tablespoon butter, and mix. Add the grated *grana* and cover. Serve *immediatamente,* with an extra supply of cheese handy, should anyone want it.

A good red wine is the perfect partner for risotto alla Milanese. Open a nice bottle of Oltrepò Pavese Bonarda around the time you start the cooking proceedings, and you'll see what we mean.

Saffron Notes

The use of saffron spreads back to a time when history dissolves into folklore. Prized by the Greeks and Romans, mentioned by Homer and Virgil, it was known by the Middle Ages as vegetable gold, and served as an international currency.

But vegetable gold, like swamp treasure,* was not originally valued as a culinary treat. Its unmistakable aroma enlivened the senses in the form of perfume. And mixed with honey, its unique flavor enhanced syrups prepared for medicinal purposes.

Saffron is made from the stigmas of the autumn crocus (*Crocus sativus*). To make just one pound of this precious seasoning, 75,000 blossoms must be

*See page 18.

gathered up! Lucky we are that minute quantities go such a long way. In Italy, saffron is sold in small $^{12}/_{100}$-gram envelopes (about the size of sugar packets), and one of these is potent enough to flavor four servings of risotto. Because they are premeasured, they are very convenient, but if you can't find them in specialty stores here, buy the saffron sold in little glass tubes.

Spanish saffron is very good. Don't substitute Mexican saffron, though. Its much lower price is due to the fact that it imparts primarily color, and very little flavor, to the dish. All right for Valerius van Diependaele's purposes, but not for ours!

A WORD ABOUT *Oltrepò Pavese Bonarda*

Across the Po River from the city of Pavia, in Lombardy, lies a large wine-producing zone with great potential and variety. Among the better-known reds is Bonarda. Dark, garnet-colored Bonarda has the rich, grapy qualities that warm your soul on an overcast day: the kind of day when you want to hole up with a good book and lounge on the couch, with a blanket thrown over your feet.

OTHER SUGGESTED RED WINES: Oltrepò Pavese Barbacarlo, Rosso, or Barbera, Narbusto, Franciacorta Rosso (all Lombardy), or Dolcetto (Piedmont).

A WORD ABOUT *Lugana*

This is a fine golden wine, delicate and dry, with undertones of flowers. Grown in an area stretching south of Lake Garda (Lombardy) into the region of Veneto, Lugana has a special freshness, recalling breezy days, cool sunlight, and lakeside walks.

OTHER SUGGESTED WHITE WINES: Tocai di San Martino della Battaglia, Franciacorta Pinot still white (both Lombardy), Albana di Romagna (Emilia-Romagna), or Masianco (Veneto).

RISOTTO LIRICO

Since early in the last century, the story of risotto has been inextricably mixed with that of opera. Indeed, the Milanese newspapers used risotto as a measuring stick for an opera's success. Hungry operagoers made it a habit to stop by the Biffi-Scala restaurant for a late-night risotto after having enjoyed an evening of music. When the Biffi was crowded early, it was obvious that the public found the lure of risotto greater than the desire to hear the end of the opera. And so it was that the headline FIRST RISOTTO SERVED AT 10:30 P.M.! (operas at La Scala usually began at nine) clearly spelled fiasco when splashed across the front page.

The name of Donizetti found its way into the annals of risotto history when it was said of him that he could write a whole cycle of songs "while the rice is cooking." Pretty fast . . . unless, of course, he was following Rossini's recipe. Not that I would ever denigrate the great master of opera buffa, but here are his original instructions—look how long the good maestro tells us to cook the rice!

> Melt ninety grams of butter with again as much strained bone marrow, then add fifty grams of rice and an appropriate amount of salt to the pot. Mix the rice until it has absorbed all the butter (this takes approximately five minutes). Next add two ladlefuls of excellent broth. Repeat the operation after another five minutes. At this time you should also add fresh mushrooms of the finest quality, cleaned and sliced.

After this, add four fresh tomatoes, cut up and with seeds removed. [You do have the option of using good tomato sauce instead.] Once again, add two ladlefuls of broth, and after letting the rice cook for about forty minutes, add twenty grams of good grated Parmesan cheese. Take the pot off the flame, and add two egg yolks to the risotto. Let the pot sit for five minutes . . . now you can serve it.

Fifty-five minutes! Phew!

I hope you got a good Rossinian laugh out of that one—we'll assume he was using brown rice (from which only the outer hull has been removed). In no other case would we attempt a variation on a great composer's theme, but we hope we won't be judged too harshly if vanity gets the better of us here. Rosario's risotto with sun-dried tomatoes follows. May the double history live on! ◆◆

RISOTTO AI POMODORI SECCHI

Risotto with Sun-Dried Tomatoes

Approximately 6–8 cups chicken stock
8 tablespoons (1 stick) butter
1 medium white onion, cut in small pieces
2 cups raw rice
¾ cup Dolcetto di Ovada wine
14–16 sun-dried tomatoes
10 leaves fresh (or 1 teaspoon dried) basil
¾ cup grated Parmesan cheese (grana)
Freshly grated black pepper to taste

On an out-of-the-way burner, bring the chicken stock to a boil. Then lower the heat and keep at a gentle simmer throughout the risotto procedure.

Melt six tablespoons (¾ stick) butter in the risotto pot. Then add the chopped onion and sauté over a low flame. As soon as it's soft and golden-tinged, add the rice and raise the flame slightly. Mix well, so the rice absorbs all the butter. When you hear the rice start to "pop," add the wine and let it sizzle away.

When the wine has evaporated, ladle over a cupful of hot stock and swirl it through the rice. After the rice has absorbed it, add the sun-dried tomatoes, stirring carefully so they don't break apart. Before the pot threatens to dry out too much, add another ladleful of stock. Stir frequently and carefully. When this, too, has been pretty well absorbed, add more stock. Continue this procedure, giving the thirsty pot adequate time to drink up the stock between ladlefuls, until the rice is almost ready.

Take the rice off the flame and add the basil (it's best to tear this into pieces by hand so as not to lose flavor on the chopping board). Stir. Then add the remaining two tablespoons butter, the grated *grana,* and freshly ground black pepper to taste. Give the pot a last mix and cover for two minutes.

Serve immediately, with a supply of extra *grana* on the table, should anyone want more cheese.

The perfect accompaniment? The remaining Dolcetto wine, poured into oversized round glasses. *Molto gustoso!**

Sun-Dried Tomato Notes

These little fellows are expensive but just bursting with flavor. You won't need many to make a statement with any dish. They are delicious sliced up in salads. They're heaven served with Belgian endive or smoked mozzarella!

The drying is effected by cutting the tomatoes in half, salting them, and letting them dry in the sun and air. Sun-dried tomatoes are available commercially in two forms: packed in olive oil or packaged dry.

Should you use the dry-packed tomatoes in risotto, make sure to soak them in water for a good hour before use, to soften them. Add the tomatoes to the risotto before you start adding stock.

When using tomatoes packed in oil, make sure you

*Very tasty indeed!

remove the excess oil before adding them. If you don't like a lot of salt, you may wish to soak these, too, in water before use.

You'll find the tomato skins, left in the risotto, curl off and separate by themselves. If you don't care for them, take them out with pincers.

A WORD ABOUT *Dolcetto di Ovada*

Yet another star from Piedmont's wine constellation, this Dolcetto, from the hills near Ovada in the southeastern Piedmont, is Rosario's favorite Dolcetto. It is sturdy and purple, soft and grapy, dry, and as bitteralmondy as an amaretto cookie. Swirl it around in your mouth to feel its robust texture. Rich as royal garb.

OTHER SUGGESTED WINES: Dolcetto D'Alba, Dol cetto di Dogliani, Gattinara, Spanna, Barbera (all Piedmont).

BORROWED FROM
BOCCACCIO

Once upon a time, there lived in Florence a simple-witted painter named Calandrino. He enjoyed going round with a group of fellow artists, who, cleverer than he, often had a little fun at his expense.

A particularly merry prankster by the name of Maso Del Saggio was the comrade responsible for the following bit of leg-pulling:

Calandrino was sitting near the altar of the Church of San Giovanni, intent at copying a painting. Maso and a fun-loving accomplice drew near and pretended they were alone. They began to discuss secrets in the kind of hoarse whisper meant to be overheard. And soon enough Calandrino got to his feet and went over to the gossiping men. They were discoursing on the virtues of various stones equipped with magical powers. The two men continued their conversation in front of Calandrino, who was all ears.

"And where do these stones come from?" cut in Calandrino, able to contain his curiosity no longer.

"Well, you'd be most likely to find them in a town called Enjoy Yourself," began Maso calmly, as he watched Calandrino's excitement grow. He embroidered: "It's quite a place to see—the vines are all tied up with sausages, and there's a huge mountain made solely of Parmesan cheese—that delectable stuff!" Maso licked his lips. "The local people spend their time making scrumptious edibles, cooking them up in capon broth and sending them rolling down the mountainside. You know, by the time they reach the bottom, they have the most perfect dusting of Parmesan cheese."

At this point, Maso looked straight at his buddy, who nodded emphatically to give more credence to the story. Calandrino was agape.

"And, well, they don't drink water there, never even heard of the stuff. The rivers flow with fine Vernaccia wine. It's a place fit for a king." Maso brought his fingers to his lips and kissed them loudly.

Now Calandrino suddenly burst out in earnest longing, like a dog who has been trying to keep still but just can't. "Where is the town of Enjoy Yourself? I must go there right away!"

"Well, it's not too close . . ." Maso began studiedly, as if to dampen Calandrino's enthusiasm.

"How many miles?" asked Calandrino.

"Hm. A million or so. Maybe more," replied Maso, enjoying himself immensely.

"And have you ever been there?"

"Me? There? My goodness—a thousand times at least!"

"Well, then, tell me, is it farther south than Rome?"

"Yes, perhaps a bit farther."

"Dear me," sighed Calandrino longingly. "That *is* far! I do wish it were nearer, so that I might go see the foodstuffs tumbling down the mountainside and snatch up my fill." He fell into silent reverie, and if Maso hadn't turned his discourse back to the virtues of those magical stones, I daresay Calandrino would still be there in the Church of San Giovanni, looking wistfully off into the distance and salivating at the thought of fine sausages, broth, Parmesan cheese, and Vernaccia wine.

For the little bit of gullible Calandrino in us all, the following recipe may be interpreted as the road map to Enjoy Yourself. ◆◆

RISOTTO ALLE SALSICCIETTE

Risotto with Sausage

> *Approximately 6–8 cups vegetarian stock*
> *4 tablespoons (½ stick) butter*
> *Freshly grated black pepper to taste*
> *1 medium white onion, cut in small strips*
> *2 cups raw rice*
> *16 ounces sweet Italian sausage meat (casing removed)*
> *1 cup Chianti Classico wine*
> *6 leaves fresh sage or 1 teaspoon dry rubbed sage*
> *Needles from three 2-inch sprigs fresh rosemary*
>   *(discard the woody center to which they are*
>   *attached) or 1 teaspoon dried rosemary (soaked in*
>   *hot water for 1 hour)*
> *¾ cup grated Parmesan cheese* (grana)

Bring the vegetable stock to a boil on a back burner, turn the heat down to very low, and keep at a simmer while making the risotto.

Melt three tablespoons butter in the risotto pot. Then add a sprinkling of freshly ground black pepper. Add onions and sauté until they lose all resistance to the touch of a wooden spoon. Mix in the rice and sausage together and sauté until the sausage appears cooked. Pour in the Chianti Classico, mix, and wait till it evaporates.

Ladle over a cupful of stock and stir well. When the rice has pretty well absorbed the stock, add a fresh ladleful and stir again. Continue this procedure until the rice is almost done—it should be tender but firm to the bite.

Fold in the sage and rosemary, and give the pot a good stir. When the rice is still a tad chewy, take it off the flame and mix in the last tablespoon butter, together with the grated *grana*. Cover for two minutes, and . . . *Ecco! Una meraviglia!**

Remember to have extra *grana* and a peppermill on the table. Ah, yes; by now the Chianti will have a good chance to breathe and, served in capacious glasses, will truly enhance the risotto.

A WORD ABOUT *Chianti Classico*

Chianti Classico comes from the heart of Tuscany, between Florence and Siena. Styles vary from medium-bodied to rich and hearty, and quality ranges from mediocre to sublime. Excellent Chianti is readily available here, and Tuscany's large output, coupled with a trend to modernize production, makes it a wonderfully affordable premium wine.

Chianti is made from the dark Sangiovese grape, along with Canaiolo, Trebbiano, and Malvasia grapes. It is drinkable in two to five years, is *vecchio* (aged) in three to seven, and is *riserva* (reserve) in four to eight. Experiment with Chianti. Discover nobility in a bottle!

OTHER SUGGESTED WINES: Other Chiantis, such as: Colli Fiorentini, Colli Aretini, Colli Senesi. Or Cabernet, Carmignano, Monte Antico Rosso, Le Pergole Torte (all Tuscany), or Decugnano dei Barbi Rosso (Umbria).

*Wow! A miracle!

A BIT OF LITTLE-KNOWN HISTORY

"Vile stuff!" exclaimed Julius Caesar, turning up his nose. "What have you got on there? Tallow?" He was criticizing a plate of asparagus served thick with butter, which thoughtful Cisalpine Gauls (the inhabitants of Lombardy in Roman times) had prepared, anxious to please their illustrious visitor.

These Gauls lacked the rights to which Roman citizens were entitled, and they dearly wished to better their lot. So they welcomed Caesar, as he seemed genuinely interested in their fate. And indeed, he was—he saw in Cisalpine Gaul a rich, thickly populated region, a great potential recruiting ground. So he flattered its inhabitants a bit, treating them almost as if they were Roman citizens.

Perhaps only reasons of politeness forced him to take a second bite of that icky mess which the Cisalpine Gauls apparently considered a delicacy. Was Northern Italian cooking really about to enter the annals of history on such a sour note?

Well, lest we jump too hastily to conclusions about Mr. Caesar's taste, let us point out that the second bite brought some major reconsiderations in its wake.

"So, asparagus can be prepared with condiments other than oil. You know, I'm starting to like this stuff. What do you call it? Butter? How's it made? Not bad."

Perhaps as a result, the citizens of nearby Lodi soon had Roman citizenship.

Asparagus with fresh butter is a pretty congenial dish in itself, but of course, those artful Northerners have improved on it since, by adding a little rice, a little broth, and a little cheese. The name of their creation? Risotto agli asparagi! ◆◆

RISOTTO AGLI ASPARAGI

Risotto with Asparagus

> 20 stalks young asparagus
> Approximately 6–8 cups chicken stock or mixed
>   chicken and meat stock
> 8 tablespoons (1 stick) butter
> 1 medium white onion, cut in ½-inch squares
> 2 cups raw rice
> ¾ cup Orvieto wine
> ¾ cup grated Parmesan cheese (grana)
> 2 leaves fresh sage (or ¼ teaspoon dried)
> Freshly grated black pepper to taste

Place asparagus stalks horizontally on a cutting block. Cut each stalk into three equal sections. Discard the tough bottom third. Add the middle third to the stock pot, bring to a boil, and let simmer for thirty minutes before starting the risotto. Keep on low heat throughout the risotto procedure. (Should you be making stock from scratch, add the asparagus to the rest of the vegetable company right at the beginning.)

If you are lucky enough to have very slender asparagus, you can use the tips whole. With thicker stalks, cut the tips in half longitudinally (or indeed in quarters, if they are quite large). Set aside.

Melt six tablespoons (¾ stick) butter in the risotto pot. Add the chopped onion and stir over low heat until the onion turns clear but has not yet begun to brown. Add the rice, raise the heat a tad, and stir to coat the rice thoroughly with the butter. Cook until the grains have taken on a jewel-like appearance. Then pour in the Orvieto and, mixing well, let it steam away. Once it has evaporated, add a cupful of stock; stir carefully so the rice doesn't stick. Before the pot gets too dry, ladle over another cup of stock and stir as before. Continue this procedure for 10–12 minutes, at which point the rice will be about half cooked. Then add the asparagus tips to the pot and carefully mix. From here on in, you must be extra careful when stirring; it would be a shame to break apart the tender asparagus tips.

Resume adding the stock, a little at a time, mixing, and waiting for the rice to absorb it. When the rice is just about done (perhaps another 8–10 minutes), add the grated *grana* with the remaining two tablespoons butter, the sage leaves, and a liberal sprinkling of black pepper. Mix a last time, and cover the pot for a two-minute repose. Serve immediately, with extra *grana* available for *chi lo desidera.**

Have the remaining Orvieto, well chilled, on the table.

Asparagus Notes

Fresh asparagus has tightly closed tips; open tips mean older asparagus and lost flavor. Choose firm, not limp, stalks.

*Whoever wishes.

Before refrigerating asparagus, trim the stem ends and wrap the cut ends in wet paper towels.

A WORD ABOUT *Orvieto*

This white wine made from Trebbiano, Verdello, Grechetto, and Malvasia grapes comes from the lovely hill town of Orvieto in Umbria (central Italy). It is crisp, dry, and golden, with a hint of fruit in its personality. Appealingly soft in texture, lightly zestful, it is perfect for a summer's day when the emphasis is on refreshment.

WINES YOU MAY SUBSTITUTE: Trebbiano (Tuscany or Latium), Est! Est! Est! (Latium), or Colli del Trasimeno (Umbria).

CINDERELLA

Once upon a time, there lived a beautiful girl, slim and exquisite, with flowing blond hair. Her real name has been lost to us, and though she later came to be known as Cinderella, for the time being I'll call her Annie.

Annie was doted on by her mother at every step. She was always made up to be perfect, dressed in expensive garments and decked out with pearls. Her mother would force her to draw in her breath and then lace up her corset till she felt her ribs were bursting. Her dazzling golden hair was brushed a thousand strokes, and fresh flowers were arranged in it each morning. The arranging could take an hour or more, as her mother was severely critical. When all went well, Annie was able to leave her room by late morning and walk solemnly about the house. Going outdoors was, of course, out of the question, as a sudden wind might come up and muss her hair.

Annie lived with her mother and a chubby step-sister named Megan, who, though forced to do many unpleasant tasks, was at least at liberty to breathe and curse as she pleased. As long as the house was clean, and dinner on the table at seven, Megan could disappear, for all her stepmother cared. Indeed, Annie's mother felt she marred the perfection of the house, which Annie's presence lit up with beauty. Annie herself, prisoner of the house and of her corset, was supremely envious, a sentiment she could never articulate, because the expression of a negative thought would have an ugly impact on her soft lips.

"Well, well . . ." mused Annie's mother one day over an elegant card in the morning's mail. "It seems the prince is giving a party . . . with the express purpose of finding a woman worthy to be his bride. Oh, Annie! This is your opportunity. I should hate to see you leave the confines of this house to live elsewhere, but in a mansion . . . the wife of the prince . . . Well, I might be able to stand it. I just might."

A seven-day crash diet was started. Eyelashes were curled, and hair was conditioned with a special styling mousse. Megan was assigned the job of hand-sewing sequins to the bodice of Annie's dress. Orchids were ordered.

At last the day arrived. Megan bleached a stripe down the middle of her own hair, then dyed it iridescent orange. She donned an oversized black blouse, tight white pants, and loud plastic sandals. "Toodle-oo!" she called, and sailed out the door. She hopped on her bicycle and rode over to the prince's.

Annie was stifling under the pounds of clothing, jewelry, and makeup which Megan had helped her put on. "Just a moment, Mother," she murmured. "I must sit down a second before we leave. I feel so tired, so faint."

"Yes, dear. Now you sit a moment and rest. I'll go on ahead and scout out the situation. I think I should present you to the prince myself. It's only fitting. I'll send the chauffeur back with the limo for you as soon as I get there. In the meantime, I'll start right in on the prince. His curiosity will already be piqued. Then the mere vision of you will be enough to make you a shoo-in!" So saying, she left.

Annie put her hand to her forehead and groaned. Her head was swimming. She longed for freedom. For the first time she admitted it.

Just then, her fairy godmother appeared. "Come, come, dear," she said. "That's no way to go to the party! The prince so hates overly-got-up girls. Here, I'll help you create the desired impression."

With the wave of a wand, Annie was dressed in jeans. Another wave, and her diamonds turned to rhinestones; her delicate slippers to sneakers; the long, gentle waves of her hair to short spikes. Then the fairy godmother gazed at her thoughtfully to consider her makeup.

Impulsively, Annie ran to the fireplace, which Megan had forgotten to clean, she'd been so busy helping Annie dress. She thrust her hands in the ashes and rubbed them over the lids of her eyes and under her cheekbones.

"Fantastic!" screamed the fairy godmother, in utter delight. "Black eyeshadow . . . black rouge! I love it! Why, you're my little Cinderella."

Annie smiled with joy. For the first time in her life, she'd expressed herself. She was raring to go.

The chauffeur arrived and opened the door of the sleek black limo. Annie drew back, frightened.

"Not to worry, my dear," exclaimed the fairy godmother. A wave of her wand, and the limo turned into a hot sports car. She handed Annie the keys. "Now, dear," she admonished, "make sure you're home by midnight, because my magic will wear off at the stroke of twelve. You'll be wearing those awful fancy clothes again, and that stuffy old chauffeur will be waiting for you in the limo!"

Annie drove off, her heart aflutter. At the door, she spied her mother, who luckily didn't recognize her. The prince needed only one look before he politely excused himself from his company and walked over. "What's your name?" he asked. "Cinderella," she answered.

Time passed. Annie glanced at the clock, and a look of horror shadowed her face. It was 11:59! She streaked past her mother, who was standing grief-stricken at the door, and dashed for her sports car. In her scramble, she stepped on one shoelace and lost a sneaker. Slam! At least she'd made it to the car.

She turned the key in the ignition and raised a dust cloud as she disappeared around the curve. By the time the prince caught up, sneaker in hand, the only vehicle to be seen was a long black limo with a stately, uncomfortable-looking girl inside.

And so he began to make the rounds with his souvenir sneaker, to see who might have the mate. Nobody seemed to know where the blonde with the great punk hairdo lived, though they had all admired her at the party. She had seemed so relaxed yet self-assured. So natural.

When he stopped at Annie's house, he almost didn't go in. Someone was being yelled at, and he certainly didn't want to step into a family argument. He turned on his heels, but a new thought brought him up short. What if *she* was in there? How could he consider his search thorough if he left out even one house? He jabbed at the doorbell.

Megan arrived quickly, cursing under her breath. "Oh, you!" she exclaimed. "Please come in. I'm in the middle of cooking risotto, which, as you know, can't be left!"

"Risotto?" asked the prince. "What kind of risotto?" He cast a hurried glance into the living room, where the quarreling was growing ever louder.

"Risotto with pumpkin," answered Megan matter-of-factly, as if there were no other varieties. "It'll just be another couple of minutes," she soothed him.

The prince breathed in the heavenly smell and sat down. He hadn't taken a bite of food since he'd been mesmerized by that unknown girl at the party, and he suddenly realized how hungry he was. Megan grated a cupful of Parmesan cheese into the risotto and stirred in a knob of butter. Then she covered it and set it to rest on the counter.

"So what can I do for you?" she asked, as she approached the prince. "By the way, I must compliment you on that bang-up party you gave. I had a great time."

"Well, that's why I'm here," he answered, most thankful that she had provided the opener. Between mouthfuls of steamy risotto, he told Megan about the mysterious girl and asked if she knew anything of her.

"Well, no," Megan answered, "although I must say there was something familiar about her. I can scout around if you'd like, and let you know if I come up with anything."

Just then, Annie's mother belted her one, and she let out an astonished wail. Until the Prince's party, her mother would never have dreamed of touching her in any way but a caress. But Annie had never let her down before.

"Here I give you a golden opportunity, and you muff it!" she screeched. "After all I've done for you! How stupid you are! How ungrateful!"

The prince squirmed uncomfortably at the violence in the next room. Megan gazed thoughtfully at her bowl of risotto. "I guess my eyes were bigger than my stomach," she commented.

"I think I shall have to punish you this time," Annie's mother hissed nastily from the living room. So saying, she reached for Megan's sewing kit and got out a pair of scissors. Slowly, but decisively, she cut off twenty-two inches of golden hair. What was left stood up in defiant spikes. "Now go put on some of Megan's clothes. See how it feels to look a slob!" she screamed. As her daughter silently obeyed, she crumpled into a sobbing heap at the thought of such beauty marred.

Annie was returning down the hall, her face puffed from crying, her eyes focused on the floor, her gait slightly uneven due to the fact that she wore only one sneaker, when she bumped into somebody. Startled, she looked up at the unexpected obstacle.

"My dear sweet Cinderella! Found at last!" cried the prince.

Megan helped prepare the wedding dinner. The prince insisted on risotto with pumpkin as a first course. Naturally, the affair was a stunning success, and he later helped Megan start a catering company.

Cinderella's mother stood repentant. Tears streamed down her face as she gazed at the couple. "I never would have imagined," she repeated over and over, as she threw Arborio rice over them. ◆◆

RISOTTO ALLA ZUCCA

Risotto with Pumpkin

> *Approximately 6–8 cups chicken or vegetable stock*
> *1 small pumpkin*
> *8 tablespoons (1 stick) butter*
> *1 medium white onion, cut in small pieces*
> *4 leaves fresh sage (or ¼ teaspoon dried)*
> *2 cups raw rice*
> *¾ cup Rosso di Montalcino wine*
> *¾ cup grated Parmesan cheese* (grana)
> *Freshly grated black pepper to taste*
> *2 tablespoons chopped fresh parsley*

Place the stock on a back burner to heat. Keep it hot, but not boiling, for the duration of the procedure.

Cut a 4-inch hole in the top of the pumpkin, and cut and remove the meat without disturbing the shell. Set the hollowed-out pumpkin shell aside.

Cut the pumpkin meat into ¾-inch cubes. You will need approximately two cups worth for the risotto. (You can make a *frittura di zucca* with the rest: Cut in flat slices, dip in egg and bread crumbs, and fry. Follow directions under Risotto al Salto, page 114.)

Melt six tablespoons (¾ stick) butter in the risotto pot over low heat. Add the onion and the sage. As soon as the onion loses its color, add the pumpkin and stir for about one minute, till all the pumpkin cubes are well glossed with butter. Mix in the rice, coating it thoroughly, too, and making sure it doesn't stick to the pot.

Next add the wine, and stir until it evaporates. Then start ladling over the hot stock, a cup at a time. Wait for the rice to absorb the liquid between cupfuls. Stir occasionally.

After about sixteen minutes, begin testing the rice for doneness. When it still has a very slight bite to it (al dente) but is tender, turn off the flame and fold in the remaining two tablespoons butter and grated *grana*. Pepper it to your liking, and sprinkle with the fresh parsley. Cover. After a two-minute rest, spoon it into the pumpkin shell and rush to the table. You're ready for a truly *fragrante* risotto!

Serve the rest of the Rosso di Montalcino in generous globe glasses.

A WORD ABOUT *Rosso di Montalcino*

Rosso di Montalcino is the younger brother of Brunello (one of the most austere, complex reds of Tuscany and all Italy). Though not aged nearly as long, Rosso still has a generous, well-rounded bouquet, a warm color and flavor. It is eminently drinkable and certainly an excellent buy.

The Sangiovese Grosso could well be joy's grape!

OTHER SUGGESTED WINES: Torgiano Rosso (also known as Rubesco), Rubino, Merlot (both Umbria), or Rosso Piceno (Marches).

New Fancies and Old Favorites

RISOTTO AI FRUTTI DI MARE

Risotto with Seafood

> 12 *large shrimp (1½ to 2 inches), or*
>   *40 fresh northern shrimp (about ½ pound)*
> *Approximately 6–8 cups fish stock*
> *8 tablespoons (1 stick) butter*
> *12 sea scallops, or 40 bay scallops*
> *12 fresh mussels*
> *1 tablespoon olive oil*
> *3 cloves garlic, crushed*
> *2 cups Verdicchio wine*
> *1 cup water*
> *1 medium white onion, cut in small pieces*
> *2 tablespoons chopped fresh parsley*
> *2 or 3 peeled ripe plum tomatoes, quartered*
> *2 cups raw rice*
> *2 tablespoons heavy cream*
> *¾ cup young grated Parmesan cheese (grana)*

Shell and devein the shrimp; add the shells to the fish stock. Let the stock simmer for a good half hour before straining through cheesecloth and discarding the shells. Then keep the stock hot, but not boiling, for the rest of the risotto procedure.

If you are using the larger shrimp, cut them in half longitudinally; northern shrimp can be used whole.

Heat one tablespoon butter in a skillet. Add the shrimp and sauté for one to two minutes until they turn pink. Shrimp cook in no time; be careful they don't get tough by overcooking them. When they have reached the desired doneness, drain them and set aside.

If you are using sea scallops, cut them in halves or quarters, depending on their size. Bay scallops may be used whole. Heat one tablespoon butter in a skillet. Add the scallops and sauté for two to three minutes or until cooked through. Keep your eye on them so you can pluck them out while they're still tender.

Wash the mussels carefully, pull or snip off their beards (the stringy black thread protruding from the shell), and check to make sure their shells are securely closed. Discard any cracked or partially opened mussels.

Heat the olive oil in a pot, add one clove of garlic, and sauté until golden. Add the mussels, one cup of Verdicchio, and the water; cover and steam for five minutes or so until the mussels have opened. Uncover to check. Scrap any that haven't opened; they are probably filled with mud.

Remove the mussels from their shells and chop gently; set aside. Discard liquid in the pot, or strain and save for mussel soup.

Melt the remaining six tablespoons (¾ stick) butter in the risotto pot over low heat. Add the rest of the garlic, together with the onion and parsley, and sauté until they start to brown. Mix in the plum tomatoes and cook until their water has evaporated. Then add the rice and stir to coat thoroughly with the tomato mixture. Splash in the last cup of Verdicchio. Mix.

Once the wine has steamed away, add the first cupful

of hot fish stock. Stir carefully to prevent the rice from sticking. Once the stock has been absorbed, add another cupful and give the pot another stir. Continue the game of add, stir, and wait, until the rice is just slightly resistant to the bite.

Add the shrimp, scallops, and mussels. Stir well to warm. Swirl in the heavy cream and follow with the grated cheese. Cover, and leave the risotto for a short *riposo** while you pour fresh, crisp Verdicchio for a well-earned toast. Keep a second bottle handily chilled.

Seafood Notes

◈ SHRIMP. Many people who live near northern coastal waters simply don't know about their own native shrimp! Available only certain times of the year, these small, nickel-sized shrimp are incredibly sweet and tender as can be. And best of all, they cost less!

When buying shrimp, look for those with close-fitting shells. Shrinkage can indicate a lack of freshness.

If you don't have a shrimp peeler, shell the shrimp by first removing the legs and tails, and then lifting off the entire covering. Or, using scissors, insert the small blade under the shell at the head, cut straight down to the tail, and peel off the shell. Remove the intestinal vein (the grayish line along the back of the shrimp after the shell has been removed) using your

*Rest.

hands, the tip of a knife, or a toothpick, under cold running water.

◈ SCALLOPS. New England bay scallops are smaller, sweeter, and more tender than sea scallops; they are also more expensive.

◈ MUSSELS. A lot of people in this country avoid mussels, for reasons unbeknownst to me. They are tender, flavorful, and plentiful on American coasts. For that reason, they are also very economical.

You can clean mussels easily with a stiff brush or plastic-mesh scrubber, under cold running water. If you find the shells slimy, scrub them with a little dry mustard first. Be sure to pull out and discard the beard.

A WORD ABOUT *Verdicchio*

Verdicchio comes from the Marches, the east-central Italian region of hills, medieval towns, and sea. The Verdicchio from Jesi is best known, but that of Matel-ica and Montanello is excellent as well. Owing to its fragility, much Verdicchio made for export is pasteur-ized or blended with other grapes, muting its flavor considerably. However, good Verdicchio can still be found here. Straw-colored, with green glints, it has a lovely, rich perfume. Its fruity, almost almondy over-tones are perfectly balanced by its dryness. So very fresh. So very fish!

OTHER SUGGESTED WINES: Torgiano Bianco (Umbria), Chardonnay (Emilia-Romagna, Tuscany, or Friuli), or Sauvignon (Emilia-Romagna, Friuli, or Veneto).

RISOTTO ALLE FRAGOLE

Risotto with Strawberries

> *Approximately 6–8 cups veal or vegetarian stock*
> *2 cups fresh strawberries*
> *8 tablespoons (1 stick) butter*
> *1 medium white onion, cut in small squares*
> *2 cups raw rice*
> *¾ cup Frascati wine*
> *¾ cup grated Parmesan cheese* (grana)
> *2 tablespoons chopped fresh Italian parsley*
> *Freshly grated black pepper to taste*
> *4–6 fresh parsley sprigs*

Bring the stock to a boil on a back burner. Then turn down the heat so the stock simmers for the remainder of the procedure.

Rinse the berries and cut off the tops. If you're using small berries, cut them in half. Larger berries should be cut in quarters. Sort through the berries and separate out the nicest ones until you have two fairly equal piles. Save the prettier berry halves for the second half of the procedure. But set aside 4 to 6 of these to use as garnishes.

Over a low flame, melt six tablespoons (¾ stick) butter in the risotto pot. Add the chopped onion, and stir gently until it has lost its color. Toss in the rice, increase the flame a bit, and mix till the grains are uniformly coated and glossy as pearls.

Then add the less pretty half of the berries. These

will break down in the cooking, adding an attractive rose color and basic tart taste to the risotto. Mix gently. Once the rice and berries have mingled nicely, add the Frascati.

After the wine has evaporated, and the pot is almost dry, pour in the first cupful of hot stock. Mix carefully to be sure the rice doesn't stick. Keep a close watch on the pot. When it is nearly dry again, add another measure of stock, and mix as before.

Continue this procedure until the rice is almost done —slightly resistant to the bite.

Before adding the last cupful of stock, mix in the remaining berries, and carefully distribute them throughout the risotto.

When the last cupful of stock has been absorbed and the rice is al dente, remove it from the heat. Stir in the last two tablespoons butter, together with the grated *grana* and the chopped parsley.

Grate black pepper over all, give a last swirl to the rice, and cover for two minutes before serving.

Crown each dish with a strawberry half. Tuck a crisp parsley sprig underneath.

An extra supply of grated *grana*, invitingly placed on the table, may well be used by more than one grateful guest.

The gently chilled Frascati completes the treat. Sheer *eleganza!*

Strawberry Notes

Wild strawberries are smaller and much more flavorful than the kind you plant yourself. If you can find them, use them whole in risotto.

When shopping for strawberries, pick those with bright-green, firmly attached caps. Brownish caps mean aging berries.

Don't wash berries before storing them in the fridge, or they'll spoil faster. Also, keep in mind that berries are very tender; if you store them too long in a high narrow container, the ones on the bottom will become mushy.

Wash the berries before you remove the caps, or the water may get inside, diluting the berries' flavor and ruining their consistency.

A WORD ABOUT *Frascati*

Frascati at once calls to mind Rome, with its plethora of *trattorie*, its generous color and constant hum. Made from a blend of Trebbiano, Malvasia, and other white grapes grown nearby, Frascati has a crisp, clean smoothness, and a medium-gold color. Frascati washes down willingly a great variety of foods. As with Verdicchio, it is not a happy traveler, and consequently much of it is subject to pasteurization, which reduces its flavor. However, good Frascati can certainly be found here.

OTHER SUGGESTED WINES: Est! Est! Est!, Colli Albani, Marino, Colle Picchioni, Fiorano Bianco (all Latium).

RISOTTO AI PIMIENTOS

Risotto with Pimientos

> *Approximately 6–8 cups chicken stock*
> *8 tablespoons (1 stick) butter*
> *1 medium white onion, cut in small pieces*
> *Freshly ground black pepper to taste*
> *2 cups raw rice*
> *¾ cup Valpolicella wine*
> *¾ cup tomato juice*
> *½ cup canned pimientos, drained*
> *¾ cup grated Parmesan cheese* (grana)
> *6 leaves fresh basil*

Bring the chicken stock to a boil on a back burner, and then turn down the flame to a whisper.

Melt six tablespoons (¾ stick) butter in the risotto pot. Toss in the chopped onions and stir until they are soft to the touch of a wooden spoon and are transparent. Give the pot a liberal sprinkling of freshly ground black pepper.

Add the rice and mix till the grains glitter with butter. Pour in the Valpolicella; stir till it evaporates. Then add the tomato juice, mixing all the while. This will give the risotto a lovely rich quality and impart a warm orangy glow.

Once the juice has been absorbed, add the first ladleful of chicken stock. Mix it evenly through the rice and wait until it, too, has been absorbed. Pour in another ladleful, stir, and wait again. Continue this pattern for the rest of the risotto procedure.

When the rice is about half done, in about 10–12 minutes, add the pimientos to the pot and mix through the rice.

As the rice nears doneness, test a grain or two. You'll want to interrupt cooking when it's still a bit al dente. Stir in the remaining two tablespoons butter, the grated *grana*, and basil leaves.

Give the pot a two-minute repose, covered, to collect these last flavors, and serve steaming hot. *Ah, che profumo!**

And bolstered with a little extra cheese, and a glass of Valpolicella . . .

A WORD ABOUT *Valpolicella*

Made up of Corvina, Rondinella, and Molinara grapes, Valpolicella is a smooth, round, fruity red produced in the hilly area around Verona, in the Veneto region. Its pretty light ruby color, medium body, and soft grapy scent make it both an eye and a palate pleaser. Some producers opt for a fuller-bodied, more velvety style, with elegant results. All in all, Valpolicella is an excellent introduction to red wines. Also, a nice summer red.

OTHER SUGGESTED WINES: Torgiano Rosso (also known as Rubesco) (Umbria), Franciacorta Rosso (Lombardy), Le Sassine, or Costa delle Pergole (both Veneto).

*Ah, what a lovely scent!

RISOTTO AI PEPERONI

Risotto with Fresh Peppers

> *Approximately 6–8 cups chicken or vegetarian stock*
> *1 yellow pepper*
> *1 red pepper*
> *1 green pepper*
> *8 tablespoons (1 stick) butter*
> *1 small white onion, cut in thin slices*
> *2 cups raw rice*
> *¾ cup Gavi wine*
> *4 sprigs fresh (or ½ teaspoon dried) oregano*
> *¾ cup grated Parmesan cheese* (grana)

Bring the stock to a gentle boil, reduce the heat, and keep it handy on a back burner throughout the procedure.

Slice the yellow, red, and green peppers into slender 2-inch strips and set aside.

Melt six tablespoons (¾ stick) butter in the risotto pot. Slide in the onion slices and let them sizzle to transparency. Then add the pepper strips and sauté for one minute.

Mix in the rice, and stir to polish well with butter. What a pot of jewels!

Add the Gavi, stir, and wait for it to bubble away. Before the pot gets too dry, pour in a cupful of hot stock and stir again. Let the rice absorb it, and then add some more. Repeat this process, mixing occasionally, until the rice approaches doneness—until it is almost tender to the bite. Now is the time to add the oregano (perhaps a little before, if you're using dried oregano).

Continue adding stock and stirring thoroughly, till the risotto is al dente; then remove from the stove and fold in the grated cheese with the remaining two tablespoons butter. Cover to retain flavor, and let repose for a couple of minutes. Serve *subito*,* with extra *grana* close behind.

The remaining Gavi, softly chilled, deserves the elegance of flute glasses.

A WORD ABOUT *Gavi*

Gavi is a world-class white, and one of Northern Italy's most fashionable wines. Made from the Cortese grape in the hills around Gavi (southeastern Piedmont), it is known for its dryness and its fresh, flinty qualities. Some examples are *frizzanti* (sparkling). Gavi has all the elegance of a Bronzino painting; it makes me think of a pale, slender-necked lady dressed in satin and pearls, or a debonair nobleman with a cool assured gaze.

OTHER SUGGESTED WINES: Favorita, Arneis (both Piedmont), Prosecco (Veneto), or Pinot Grigio (Friuli or Veneto).

*Right away.

RISOTTO AL PROSCIUTTO E PISELLI

Risotto with Italian Ham and Peas

> *Approximately 6–8 cups beef stock or*
>   *mixed-meat stock*
> *6 tablespoons (¾ stick) butter*
> *1 medium white onion, cut in thin slices*
> *Fresh garden herbs to taste (marjoram and thyme*
>   *are nice), or ¼ teaspoon each dried marjoram and*
>   *thyme leaves*
> *1 cup prosciutto, sliced ⅛ inch thick and cut in*
>   *1-inch by ¼-inch strips, leaving any fat attached*
> *1 cup peas, shelled (if you don't have fresh peas,*
>   *use frozen rather than canned; they keep their*
>   *shape and consistency better)*
> *2 cups raw rice*
> *¾ cup Pelaverga wine*
> *¾ cup grated Parmesan cheese* (grana)
> *Freshly grated black pepper to taste*

Bring the stock to boil on a back burner, then turn down the heat and let simmer for the rest of the procedure.

Over a low flame, melt four tablespoons (½ stick) butter in the risotto pot. Throw in the sliced onions and garden herbs, and stir continuously until the onion has lost its color. Mix in the prosciutto slices and cook until all the fat is melted.

If you are using fresh peas, now is the time to add them. (Frozen peas go in toward the end.)

Add the rice and raise the heat to give them a good "toasting." Mix carefully, making sure the rice doesn't stick, as it's so tempted to do at this point.

Next, with the addition of the wine, the pot will give a steamy hiss. Continue stirring till the rice threatens to stick again. Counter by ladling in a cupful of hot stock; mix until it is absorbed, and add some more. Never let the pot dry out; rescue by adding a cupful of hot stock. The rice will have a creamy consistency as it absorbs the broth.

Test the risotto for doneness when you are about to add the fifth cup of broth. When the rice is just slightly resistant to the bite, add the peas, if you have not already done so.

After another cupful of stock the air should be full of promise. Once this stock is absorbed remove the pot from the flame and stir in the remaining two tablespoons butter, the grated *grana*, and black pepper.

Cover the pot for a couple of minutes, then serve immediately.

Don't forget to have extra cheese, pepper, and of course Pelaverga available at the table, for this is a dish for someone who is truly a *buona forchetta!**

Pea Notes

Plump, bright green pods promise sweet peas; pale or yellowish ones tend to be starchy.

*Literally, good fork—someone who loves to eat.

Before shelling peas, wash their pods. The addition of the pods to the stock pot is a flavor enhancer. (Use about half the pods, tied in cheesecloth for easy removal.) If you're making stock from scratch, remove the pea pods after a half hour or so.

To separate frozen peas from one another before you open the box or bag, hit all four corners of the container firmly on a countertop.

Prosciutto Notes

You can find prosciutto in Italian markets and delis. Importation of meat products from Italy is not yet allowed, but Canada produces some excellent prosciutto. Domestic prosciutto is readily available and can be quite good. Westphalian ham may be substituted in a pinch.

Learn to recognize good prosciutto by its pinkish-red color. It shouldn't be too dark. Avoid especially fatty-looking or off-color meat. Iridescent traces indicate spoilage.

A WORD ABOUT *Pelaverga*

This is a young wine, full of verve and with a richness surprising for its tender age. It has a remarkable spicy quality, very much like currants and cinnamon, and a friendly red color. The kind of wine that can jazz up an evening. From Piedmont.

OTHER SUGGESTED WINES: Valtellina (Lombardy), Lambrusco D.O.C. (Emilia-Romagna), Bonarda (Lombardy or Emilia-Romagna).

WHAT TO DO WITH LEFTOVER RISOTTO

At one time or another, even those of us who don't believe in moderation admit, "I guess my eyes were bigger than my stomach." We offer two solutions to this very human problem of misjudgment. You may, however, find our proposals so inviting that you'll discover yourself making too much risotto on purpose.

The dishes on the following pages are ideal for snacks, light lunches, or appetizers. ❖❖

RISOTTO AL SALTO

Italian Risotto Patties

PREPARATION TIME: 20 minutes

YIELD: 9 patties

YOU WILL NEED 2 bowls, a nonstick pan, a wooden spatula or flat wooden spoon (metal may break patties), wax paper, and paper towels.

3 eggs
1½ cups finely ground bread crumbs
3 cups leftover risotto
1 teaspoon milk
Freshly grated black pepper to taste
3–4 tablespoons butter
½ teaspoon dried sage (optional)
Lemon wedges

Add two eggs and ½ cup bread crumbs to the leftover risotto. Mix well. Form patties approximately 3 inches across and 1 to 1½ inches thick. (If you make the patties too thick, the insides will not cook.) Set aside.

In one bowl beat the remaining egg together with the milk and some fresh pepper.

Place the rest of the bread crumbs in another bowl.

With your right hand, pick up the patties one at a time, put into the bowl with the egg mixture, and turn to coat evenly. Transfer the patty to the bread-crumb bowl, using your left hand, and turn until it is evenly coated. (By keeping your hands separate, you won't get crumbs in the egg bowl.) Arrange the coated patties on wax paper.

Place three tablespoons butter in a nonstick pan over medium heat. If you have a little dried sage on hand, add ½ teaspoon or so to the melted butter—it gives a lovely flavor.

Once the butter is melted (it should be bubbling but not burning), slip a few of the patties in the pan. Be careful not to overcrowd the pan, because you need room to turn the patties.

After browning the patties for a couple of minutes, turn them over gently, using a wooden spatula. When the patties are golden brown on both sides, remove from the pan and place on paper towels to drain the fat.

If your pan is not big enough to make all the patties at the same time, or if you're making a large amount, you may want to store the freshly sautéed ones in a low oven until you're ready to serve them. If you want to make them ahead of time—as for a party—you can keep the patties warm, at very low heat, for a couple of hours.

If you sauté more than one batch, add a tablespoon more of butter to each batch, to make up for the fat that the preceding patties absorbed.

When you serve the patties, place a freshly cut lemon wedge alongside. Not only does it look nice, but the

touch of sour complements the rich patties wonderfully.

◆ VARIATIONS: If the risotto you're using as a base is
not too rich, you may want to stuff the insides of the
patties with cheese. You can add a little ball of mozzarella or cheddar. Or you might try grating a little
grana on top of the patties a minute before they are
ready.

RISOTTO AL FORNO

Oven Risotto

YOU WILL NEED a cake pan of a size so that when the risotto is spread over the base, it will be about one inch thick. (Choose a square pan if uniformity is important so the risotto can be cut into even squares once cooked. Risotto baked in a round pan can be cut in wedges, though they may break more easily.)

Butter
Bread crumbs
Leftover risotto

This is much easier than making the rice patties, and it will let you go about your business while it quietly bakes.

Grease the cake pan generously with butter and sprinkle bread crumbs evenly over the bottom. Fill with leftover risotto, a handful at a time. Pat the risotto down gently as you fill the pan, being careful not to disturb the butter–bread-crumb coating on the bottom, or else the rice may stick. Use a tall straight glass or a small rolling pin to flatten the risotto evenly. Dot the top with dabs of butter, or with a little melted butter. Sprinkle bread crumbs over all and bake on top shelf of a 450-degree oven for about 40 minutes, or until golden brown. Cut into pieces and serve. Grate a little *grana* over all, if desired.

A NOTE ON
IMPROVISATION

Because we believe that a cookbook should be a springboard for your imagination and not a series of strict, ironclad rules, we encourage you to improvise and play around with the ingredients you have on hand. The few particulars we insist upon are not born of snobbery but will only help you avoid problems. As long as you start with fresh ingredients, and don't take shortcuts that the chemistry of cooking makes counterproductive, you will come up with something interesting. Good raw materials. Simple cooking procedures. No unnecessary frills. That's what Italian cooking is all about. ◆◆

Index

**PER UN
BUON RISOTTO
OCCORRONO:** *del riso*

del burro

del vino secco

del formaggio

*una buona pentola
e del brodo*

un cucchiaio di legno

**PER UN
BUON RISOTTO
OCCORRONO:** *del riso*

del burro

del vino secco

del formaggio

*una buona pentola
e del brodo*

un cucchiaio di legno